# the Jim Odrich *Experience*

Fly Me To The Moon
The Girl From Ipanema
What Is This Thing Called Love?
Prisoner Of Love
Triste
That's All
The Coffee Song
Misty
If I Should Lose You
Once Upon A Time

3062

Printed in Canada

MMO CD 3062

**Music Minus One**

# The Jim Odrich Experience
## Pop Piano Played Easy

# Fly Me To The Moon

Words and Music by Bart Howard

The intro features drums and bass alone to set a tasty jazz flavor.  Piano then enters with melody, at first simply, then with a variety of textures ending with a descending figure in block chord style.  Note how, after the band's jazz oriented figures, the piano returns with a variety of textures from phrase to phrase to maintain interest.  The invitation to end with the well-known classic "Basie Ending" is too much to resist!

6

# The Girl From Ipanema

Words and Music by Vinicius De Moraes and A. C. Jobim

The intro establishes the Bossa Nova feel with guitar, trombone and rhythm section. This very attractive Latin rhythm traditionally has the piano playing single note figures. Although the piano has the option to deviate from this, I chose to stay with this established mode, simply because it seemed best. A few well-placed LH chords help to add spice and rhythmic interest. The playing remains stylistically consistent, simple and uncomplicated to the end.

# What Is This Thing Called Love

Words and Music by Cole Porter

Flute with orchestra and rhythm section are featured in the intro. Piano next plays melody sprinkled with very sparse fills, and then changes to elaborated melody in contrasting textures. At two points during the bridge, I imitate background figures and use them as springboards into the ensuing lines. This is a good device that makes for natural continuity. In similar fashion, piano leads into the last phrase with an ascending figure that imitates a descending orchestral figure. Notice how the piano mimics the harmonic structures of the orchestra here as well as its linear movement. Flute and strings play the ending section. The piano ends the piece with an ascending arpeggiated line.

# Prisoner Of Love

Words and Music by Leo Rubin, Russ Columbo and Clarence Gaskill

The very dramatic, heavy symphonic nature of the orchestra's introductory statement, ending with a majestic sweep up to the lead-in chord, leaves no doubt as to what the piano must do. I begin with symphonic voicings and follow the free-time pace set by the orchestra. When the rhythm section enters to establish tempo, the piano continues with an appropriately lighter symphonic flavor. Listen to the variations in texture, the changes of register, the improvisations which preserve the essential outlines of melody, as well as those which depart radically from it.

Lyrics:
A-lone, from night to night, you'll find me
Too weak to break the chains that bind me
I need no shackles to remind me
I'm just a pris-'ner of love.

18

20

# Triste

Words and Music by Tom Jobim

After a repeating rhythmic bossa-nova guiter figure supports an overlay of woodwinds, piano enters at the chorus with melody in sixths, and then changes to various textures for contrast. I then play around the melody with idiomatic pianistic configurations typical of the bossa-nova style. Flute and keyboard play a section with the arranger's "written improvisation" based on the chords of the first sixteen bars of chorus. Piano then re-enters with pianistic elaborations and figurations as before, and seizes the opportunity near the end to improvise over a repeating band figure that fades out to silence.

MMO CD 3062

# That's All

Words and Music by Alan Brandt and Bob Haymes

The lush woodwinds with strings of the intro lead to the chorus where piano plays above the supporting strings in free time. At the bridge, I change the mood somewhat with improvisation around the melody. The remainder of this piece features a variety of contrasting textures such as a single-note melody with arpeggiated bass, and a switch to upper register at one point to match the strings. After the ritard into the ending, I play a variation of an ascending scalewise passage to the end. At the very end, piano plays an ascending figure as its final statement.

# The Coffee Song

Words and Music by Bob Hillyard and Dick Miles

At the intro, the band establishes an exciting Latin-jazz feel for the entire piece. After playing the obligatory melody during the first eight bars of the chorus, the piano accepts the sustained strings' invitation to stretch out a bit with a jaunty improvisation in the same happy mood. At the bridge, the rhythmic trombone figures ask for melodic simplicity. The piano complies in order to maintain sonic clarity. After the bridge, the background once again permits me to return to free improvisation, as does the key change after the exciting big band section.

MMO CD 3062
The Coffee Song - 1

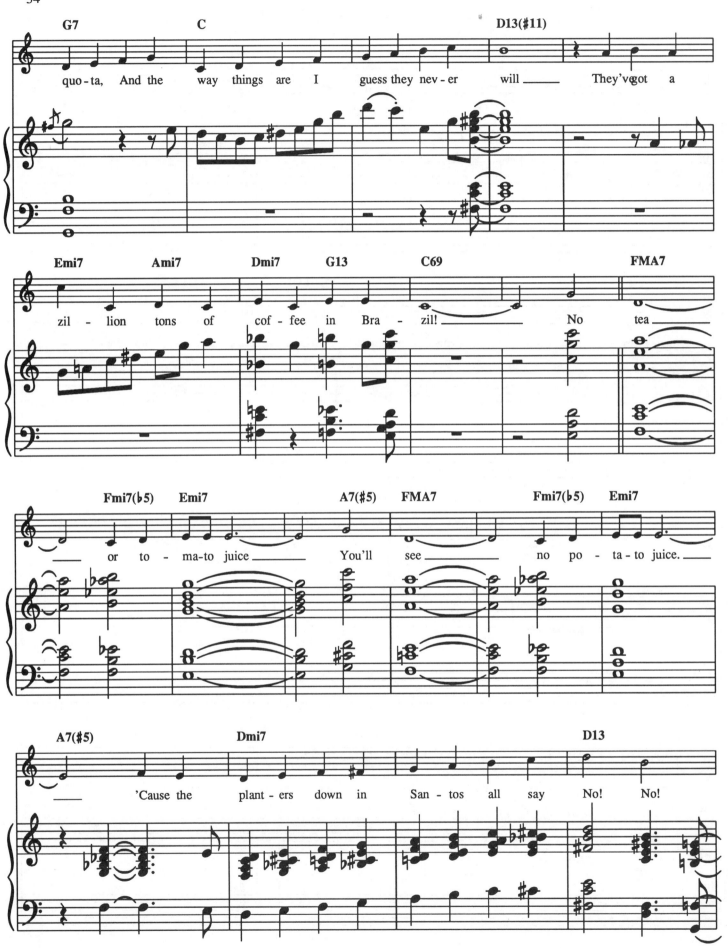

# Misty

Words and Music by Johnny Burke and Errol Garner

Since this arrangement starts with a piano pickup into the first bar, there is a two-beat count off. The piano goes directly to melody with varied textures. I keep referring to the frequent changing of textures and registers because this is a good way to keep your playing moving forward without getting stuck in the deadly groove of sameness. During the second eight bars, the piano performs a stylistic elaboration of melody (with an understated hint of Errol Garner's patented RH inner voice motion since his was the well-known definitive recording). At the bridge, after the orchestra states the first four bars of melody, the piano answers appropriately in much the same manner as spoken conversation. This alone serves as a fresh change to catch the listener's ear. Since the very lush orchestral extended ending is beautiful by itself, I chose to stay out of it, remaining true to the notion that we should always opt for what is musical, natural, graceful and contextually appropriate.

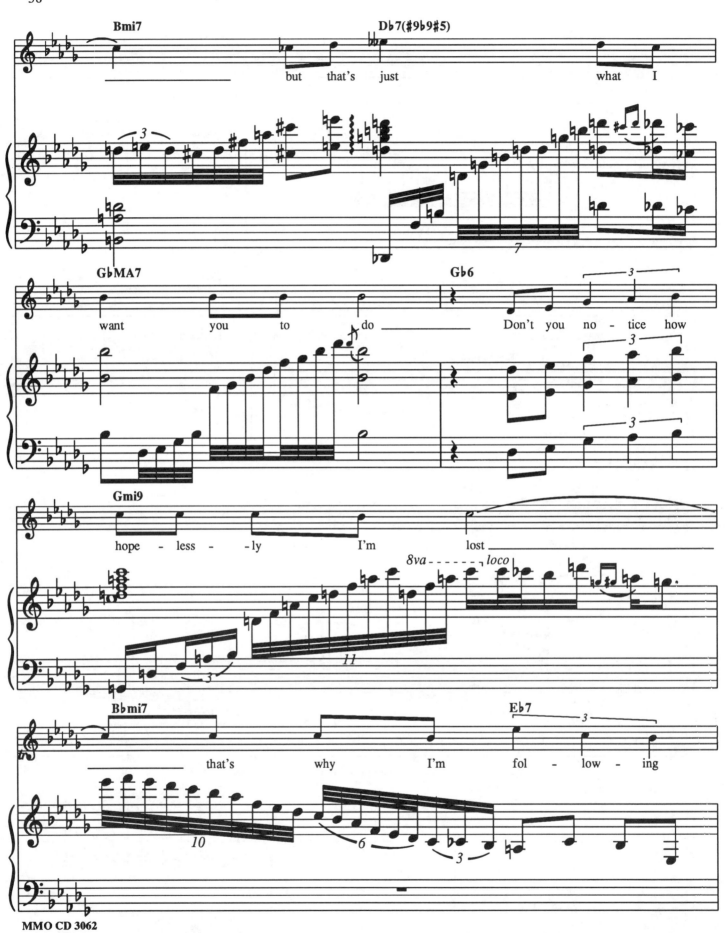

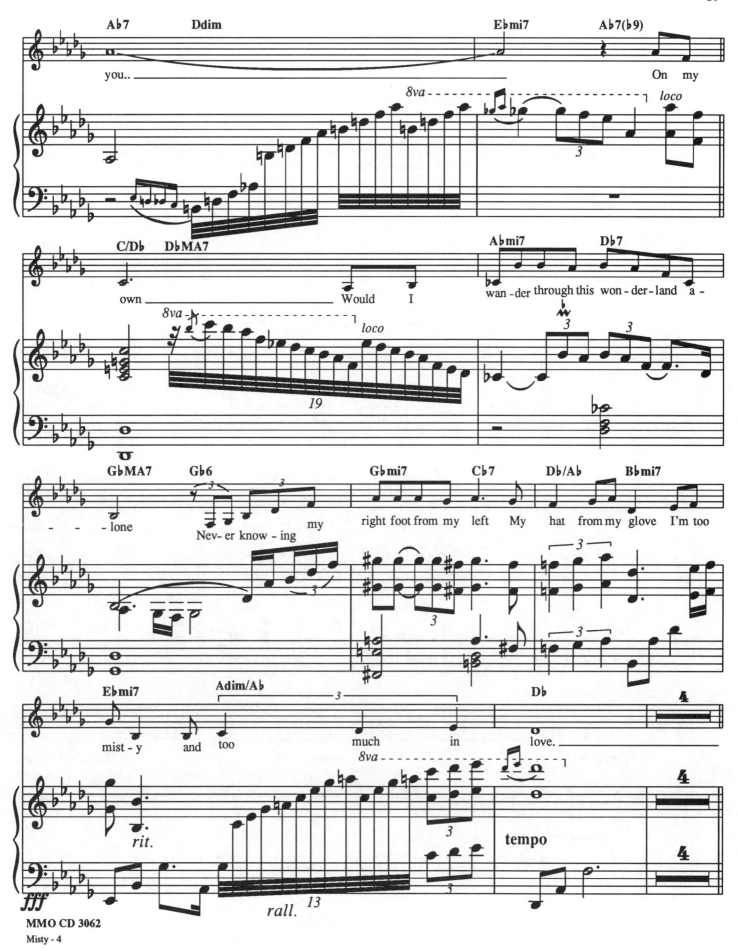

# If I Should Lose You

Words and Music by Ralph Rainger and Leo Robin

The intro features exciting jazz to preface what is to come. The piano, wishing to establish melody, and also to pace its expenditure of melodic and rhythmic energy, resists the impulse to bang away with a frenzied jazz improvisation. Instead, I opt for contrast via a variety of melodic textures in a somewhat restrained extension of the same style as the background. During the second phrase, though, the piano picks up the pace a bit with light improvisation around the melody, and lets a few background figures sound through. You will do this if you listen not only to yourself, but to the combined sound of solo and background. For the rest of this piece, listen to the constant use of textural and stylistic variation, for these go a long way toward making your playing sparkle. Notice how the ending piano figure modifies the classic "Basie Ending," again to add a bit of flair as a surprise which helps to avert the boredom of total predictability.

42

vain, if I ev - er lost you. ____

# Once Upon A Time

Words and Music by Strouse and Adams

The intro features lush strings and woodwinds that set the mood.  The piano appropriately enters with light varied textures, and continues into the next phrase with slightly fuller voicings.  Notice how at the bridge, the piano, in an almost stalking way, cautiously follows the orchestra's free movements and plays along in such a way as to enhance, but not interfere.  The piano's more chordal textures in the final phrase provide needed contrast here.  The ending employs single note improvisation that follows and supports the graceful final statements of lush strings.

# the Jim Odrich *Experience*

Fly Me To The Moon
The Girl From Ipanema
What Is This Thing Called Love?
Prisoner Of Love
Triste
That's All
The Coffee Song
Misty
If I Should Lose You
Once Upon A Time

**3062**

**MMO Music Group • 50 Executive Boulevard, Elmsford, New York 10523, 1-(800) 669-7464**
Website: www. minusone.com • E-mail: mmomus@aol.com